Sicktowne

By Casimir Chotkowski, M. S. Ed., M.S. S.B.L

and

Alemapyk Sodoh

Foreward

This book is for the have nots, the under appreciated, and the unknowns. None of us ever thought we would be one of these people. We all started out new and turned out old, regardless of how much money we ended up with. The content of this book is fiction. All towns are the same really, someone is running something, somewhere because someone has to.

The book is for my children who spent one year living with me in our own type of Sicktowne. Thank you for your love and support. I will always miss the beautiful years I spent with you. Please remember the happy times we had together.

Casimir
Chotkowski

Chapter 1

At the bar

The group filled the bar, elbow to elbow. The 100 or so 30 to 50 year old white males were angry. No one had hired them in months and the town was building a 6 story housing complex—"The Linen Building." These were the local boys, sons of the bay Clammers. The Great South Bay clamming industry on the South Shore of Long Island was worn out by their Fathers and they, like them were left to make a living with their hands. The boats were all still in the back yards, wooden ships preserved in plastic, like mummified witnesses to a bye gone age. They came in off the water and in one generation had tamed the land. Their Fathers never lived through anything like this! No work, no jobs, no food for their families. Most of them had inherited their houses, no mortgage to pay, but in the last 10 years their taxes had doubled, sometimes tripled upwards! —coming close to $20 thousand dollars a year for a 2 bedroom house with almost no land. Who could afford that? - even in a strong economy. They all knew why they were here—like one particularly nasty Immigrant said as he spit into their faces, "We got Whitey on the run!" And the boys knew it. A Tsunami of Immigrants had moved into the county in the last 3 years. There was almost no place left for them to get decent wages. The local big box home improvement stores were their last outpost. Even the guys who had their own trucks and their own Dads to work with were coming into the stores now. No more stringers, independent contractors, handyman vans. You either joined up or were shut out. These guys were here to do something about it! A "We're taking it back!" mentality. They considered themselves to be the last of the great individuals. Like Hoffa starting over again, another wave of angry working men were going to organize in 2014. But Hoffa never had a cell phone, and because of that small piece of technology, these guys could be in constant contact. Organizing as a union was a ridiculous old-school notion. There was no chance for that, now that you could hire 3 immigrants for the price of one white man. They were organized as a "Thug Union." They had to cull from the neighborhoods like their Fathers and Grandfathers had culled from the Bay, each house was its own clam bed. One guy would "rake through" a neighborhood. A lone stringer, taking inventory of what he saw at street level. The roof, the shingles, the doors and windows, the trees, the landscaping the driveway for cement work. The checklist covered the essentials. Gas rising past $5.00 a gallon did not make it any easier on the fat pick-up truck drivers. Unemployment did not exist for guys like these. They employed themselves. No work, no eat. That's how it always was. The pick-up truck would make 2 or 3 passes to get all the information on the address. The guys would "focus" on the house for a year—or for as long as it took to get the owners attention, to get them to plunk down the cash to the big box fix-it up store so they would hire that guys crew. They'd take the time to follow the homeowner everywhere they went, until "the Mark" woke up and noticed that they needed repairs on their house. He didn't know that his mortgage bank owned the big box Home dispatch store. The big box store owned his mortgage. He better keep the house nice or they'd start in on his family! It was getting to be Winter soon so the guys usually turned in their tool belts for driving gloves. The oil burners were stoking up and oil had to be delivered regularly as the weather got colder. This year, a lot of the old timers retired, they sold their oil companies to the highest bidder, and the highest bidders were Immigrants. The Greenhorns who had worked at 3 jobs for the last 20 years and got their entire family jobs as well, could now afford to be the owner of their own business. They had enough money and could buy up any one of the foreclosed houses that the white boys lost to a mortgage broker when things went sour and they'd step right into the guys' life—wipe him away, just like that. These guys weren't going to let that happen to their lives. They were taking their time at the bar, unwinding from another day of scratching out a living. No real work, just the work of beating down a homeowner to get their business. Each "crew" had claimed their 5 feet at the bar and a pitcher on tap didn't last long. They were getting restless and loud as "the Advisor" walked in. The Mayors Advisor was the oldest son of the oldest family in town. He knew everyone. His family had its name on the very first bronze plaque that was ever laid down in the first park near the first tree ever planted. Every family in the town owed his family a favor, one way or the other. He wasn't a blue blood, he was 5th of 6th generation off the boat and his family still had the memories of how hard it was to start out new in this country. He had deliberately skipped this tradition as he raised up his own sons. He felt that by now he had the right to call himself an American even though he bore the very ethnic sounding name of his great great grandfather. He had chosen Waspish sounding names for his sons, only their middle names betrayed their heritage though, he conceded that much to his family; though they couldn't run from the ethnicity of their family name. Until recent years, his whole life had revolved around socializing at weddings and funerals, sometimes resolving an inner family dispute and hosting the annual Christmas party where the highlight was delivering presents to the little kids on the back of a donkey. How things had changed over the last 5 years! Even gambling was down. He wasn't ready for the onslaught when he came through the door to face the more than 100 working men who believed he was their Savior. A loud roar! went up when they saw him, he jumped a little, startled by the unusual outburst from the normally stoic men. It seemed as if they were beating at him with their heavy handed slaps on the back. He knew it was all an act. They had loved his Father and Grandfather in a different way. Words like "loyalty" and "brotherhood" came to mind. He got labeled a "pretty boy," a "lightweight." He didn't mind, he never had to do any real work in his life. His Father was the task master who made him learn to work with his hands. He always waited for the big jobs to come along, then pressed him, as a boy into spending his Summers' with his "crew." He could fix, build and take apart anything that you could make money off of on a property. It all stopped at 18 when he went to college for Business Management and learned to do the work to make his money with his mind. Manual labor never occurred to him after he was tapped to come on board with the local Politicians as the Mayors Advisor and he kept the job for the next 20 years. The Mayor was just a figurehead in town and everyone knew that "the Advisor" called the shots. This time he would have to get into the thick of it with the guys and there wasn't any easy solution. He was already doing business with many of the new immigrant owners. They worked just as hard as any of the guys in the room, and they had no arrogant swagger of entitlement. In many ways they were *easier* to negotiate with, they knew the bottom line-- after living at it for the past 20 years.

Chapter 2

"Art House"

The Advisor was pacing across the polished grey concrete floor, waiting for his speechwriter to arrive. "Another evening at the circus," he thought as he saw a small woman approaching. She was carrying a large canvas and when she saw him on the other side of the gallery she scurried over like a small rodent. He put on his biggest political smile and tried to think of an appropriate comment for the childlike scratches on the canvas. "How creative!" he blurted out. She looked up at him appreciatively, "I'm hanging it right behind you, next to the green canvas," she answered politely, pointing to the blank space on the wall. "Hurry," he said, "we're going to start in 15 minutes." Another Artist had come over and was helping her nail the painting up. "Hideous!" he thought to himself, my dog paints better than that." He moved on to stand with the building Super in his office.

Safely away from the slightly erratic Artists that were gathering near the rows of black metal chairs. The Super looked up from his paperwork and extended a hand to the Advisor. "Overtime, just overtime for me." he stated flatly. The Advisor shook his head, "yep, I wish I could clock in for these things, I'm always being dragged over here for someone." His "someone" had just walked in the door and was heading his way. He gave him a small wave and hurried over to greet him with a speech typed up for this evenings event. "I've got some bright and sweet wine with me, that should take the edge off of things," he whispered in his ear. "It's always a pleasure to see my favorite Trustee," he called out, loud enough for anyone within a 10 foot radius to hear. They stepped out of the office together and headed for the long table that was set up to the left of the group of chairs. His Assistant was already setting up cups and napkins, and bringing out the wine and cheese platters that she had put together for the gathering.

It was hard to believe that this was the one year anniversary of the opening of the building. There were slightly more than half of the original (local) residents left, the other half were imported from Manhattan. He expected less than half of the building to participate. It had been a fun year to start things off and most of it was spent focusing on the Mayors re-election campaign. It was an easy win, his only opponent was a low income resident of the Art building with no political support in the town. The Advisor was "homegrown," born and raised in the town, he had announced "I'm going to be the Mayor someday" to his low income classmates when he turned 10 at the local elementary school. His prediction almost came true and he owed a lot of favors for it. In the politics of the town he was a relative newcomer and his first appointment shocked him. The Mayor had run against one of the other "ancient families" in the town. The ancient families had been running the town ever since it was formed as a strip of 3 stores on an old Indian trail that ran the length the county. More than 200 years ago. He had grown up in it when it was a slum like wreck, full of buildings from the nineteen thirties that were on the verge of collapse. He had watched the mob money slowly creep in over the years to revitalize one area at a time. He had been lucky enough to still be the Mayors Advisor just 4 years before the big money arrived and pushed with him to build the Linen Building, a 6 story luxury apartment complex in the middle of the once thriving town. The payoff would make him a millionaire. It was being built by the most corrupt conglomerate of builders that he had ever seen. There wasn't anything he could do about it or that he wanted to do about it. He was only going to be the Mayors Advisor for another 3 years, after that he had his own life to plan for. Over the past year, the local guys all saw the building going up, He knew this meeting could easily turn into his wake if he couldn't turn the tide. It was community relations at its best because almost everyone in the Art House had a relative in the building industry. He had spent the past 3 weeks meeting with every single participant in the building and he had made enough room in the budget to hire the local group for the next year. The building would be done and he would be leaving office, hopefully they would go for the plan. If they didn't everybody could go and try to find grocery money elsewhere. That much he was sure of.

Chapter 3

Money Tree

While the Advisor made his way down the bar,
stopping to exchange jokes and comments, Jack
was at the other end. "Let him come to me." He
thought out loud. His partner guffawed, "That's
right, he knows we can still take care of that 6
story box he's building." The longer the Advisor
was in the bar, the noisier it became as the group,
drinking beer and boilermakers for an hour now
worked themselves into a pep rally. "These guys
are desperate," thought the Advisor. "Nobody who
works during the week drinks this hard on a
Monday night!" Times were tough for this group,
there was not one licensed Contractor in the group.
They learned their "trade" from their Fathers,
handed down but never licensed. He had
deliberately scheduled it for a Monday so it would
go calm and short. No such luck. The crowd was
working his arm, shaking his hand hard and every

third man stared him down and stated "you're gonna take care of us right Advisor?" "Oh my God! You gotta be kidding!" he shouted back, keeping things light was critical to his plan. "Okay boys!" he shouted as he finally reached the far end of the bar. It took a minute but the dull roar became a hush. He made a point of waiting for that initial hush, then he grabbed Jack by the hand and held it up high of his head. "This is the guy you got to thank for shaking the money tree!" Jack burst into his best money maker smile. "Jack of all Trades," everybody called him because he started working when his Father was killed on a job site when Jack was just 13. He took his Fathers place and he could work in any job, doing anything on any construction site. He was planning to step in as Mayors Advisor next and he needed all the help he could get. He was from a poor white trash family and he had made a lot of enemies as he rose up through the ranks. Most of the "decent" people in town flat out hated his Father and the other families (or anyone with a daughter) hated his Brother. Not an easy shadow to get out from under. He had had more than his share of beatings and he knew he would have had a better life if he had left this town straight out of High School. He chose to stay to be with his Mother for the last 2 years of her life and after she passed away he stopped trying to get out. He wasn't the smartest guy in the room but he had gathered enough friends over the years and they needed him to win the Advisors job to swing the tide away from the immigrant wave that was pushing in to overtake all the jobs in the town. The Advisor dropped his arm and took his first step towards the door. His plan was to tell them exactly what they wanted to hear as he made his way back down the bar and straight out the door. "We got jobs for ya!" he shouted out to the crowd, he waited as the "Woo Hoo's!" died down. "Now I know it's been a tough year but everybody and I mean tell your friends—everybody who wants to work should come on down to the Linen site this Friday at 8 am. You'll sign up and get all the work that you and your crew can handle." More Woo Hoo's! and cheers went up from the crowd. He was halfway down the bar now (" Halfway home!" he thought to himself.) "How much work you got left on that shoe box Advisah?—getting close to being done ain't ya?" shouted one of the tall burly men. He recognized the man as Walter, a local he went all the way through school with. He was annoyed that one of his own was looking to cut him down. He'd remember that guy when it came time to divvy out the jobs. "We got plenty of work to carry you through the Winter --and it's indoor work boys! We built an underground parking garage and we do all the preliminary work down there, so no standing in the sub-zero this year." More cheers and Walter handed him a boilermaker, back pedaling for his off the cuff remark. He knew the Advisor from Kindergarten and he had seen him do a few really rotten things, he did not want to get

on his bad side—now or ever. "Now you did it!"
the Advisor was fuming on the inside. Walter
knew it because the more angry the Advisor was,
the bigger his smile grew. "Hey, gimme that back
Advisah!! Walter threw his arm around the
Advisors head and pretended to bend him forward
in a head lock! He grabbed the boilermaker and
downed it. The Advisor was all about the joke and
he pretended to throw a punch into Walters gut.
"This is going great! Let me get the hell out of
here," the Advisor thought with a chuckle. "Okay
guys you all gotta get up early so get on home! I
gotta go over to the site to stay on 'em so they
make room for "my boys." he shouted over the din
that had developed over his antics with Walter. He
turned to bolt towards the door and was out on the
street before the guys could stop pounding on
Walters back. He hurried down the dark sidewalk
with his head down as he dashed around the corner
he glanced up at the huge white clock hanging
over the corner of Jane Street. It was getting late

and he was looking forward to seeing his "sweetie pie"—the sweetest thing he ever laid eyes on.

Chapter 4

Was it the feeling of time passing that made her feel uneasy and dejected? She couldn't put her finger on it. She was happy for her beautiful daughter, starting out—just 18! She was sad for herself to lose her so young. Her daughter had been out in the world of adults since she was 15 so she was worldly beyond her years. Still, Lady could never feel completely happy about all of the Mother-daughter days that she was being robbed of. She realized that the uneasy feeling came from knowing and not being able to reconcile herself to the fact that every member of her family was being manipulated. The events as they unfolded felt like the ebb and flow of any average life but she knew that they were all planned events. She was never able to find out who was planning them. She knew it was someone who knew her well and who wanted to destroy her happiness. Why? She hadn't intentionally done anything wrong to anyone. She believed the reason was that she was too happy. They ruined her family because it could be ruined. The first six months were agonizing to her, her daughter had been behaving strangely, angry with her all the time. The next 6 months were excrutiating as one by one her friends old and new stopped returning her phone calls. She watched her other children being moved around like pawns. Even the Teachers at the High School were involved somehow. She had gone over the list of everyone she knew. Then she had to look at the last group of people who she had met in "Sicktowne." She called it "Sicktowne" because she knew the forward plan for the place and every person involved in it was a Sicko. She had seen her share of horrors down in that cesspool! Every town has its own home grown corruption but Sicktowne had its own murdering hunting party. Five years ago a group of High Schoolers (we're talking teenagers!) were caught roaming the streets gang hunting for Immigrants, it went on for years until finally one of the Immigrants was killed. That sent a mighty strong message out to the local community—it was changing over ever so slowly from 98% white to 60% and rising Immigrant. The Police turned a blind eye. She had been working part time at "Sicktowne" High School when it happened and she had overheard a group of the wealthiest kids in town saying it was the Fathers of the kids that got caught who arranged for the hunting parties. The other information she got was that the group of Fathers who organized it were all members of "the oldest organization in the town." That explained why the Police never followed up on the Immigrant complaints. She remembered thinking "I bet they're proud of themselves now." They had set it up so that the kid who got the worst jail sentence was the poorest one without any support from his parents. The old formula for Sicktowne, no money, no family, no power. Even though she wasn't an Immigrant, the way that her life was being systematically dismantled reminded

her of the methods of the oldest group in town--
and of the newest—an Art group "The **P**eoples **A**rt
Covenant" they called themselves-"a pack of
animals" she thought to herself. They were so
corrupt that they had Police presence at their
public meetings. Sicktowne tax dollars at work.
They were using the sick methods of the
recovering alcoholic/addict. "Pure trash is running
that organization—more sickos from Sicktowne"
she thought out loud. It was a big part of why she
tolerated so much from the Advisor. He was the
man to know around town and she needed
powerful friends to survive. She came from 100%
certified white trash, but she was born looking like
Anna Nicole Smith and the Advisor just could not
resist that kind of stunner. She giggled as she
remembered seeing him trip over a can of paint
over at the Art building the first time he ever saw
her. She knew she had him right then and there.
That was six years ago and it had been a wild ride
with him ever since that day. She threw open her

mirrored closet door and ran her hands over the peach colored cashmere sweater dress she was wearing that evening. It had clung to all of her curves and in the front it draped all the way down to her belly button. That man never had a chance. Her 40 LL's beamed right at him as she leaned over to offer him a hand to stand him up. He would have crawled right into her dress if they weren't surrounded by about 10 of his wife's best friends! She knew the Advisors wife, everybody did. A beautiful older woman, just one year younger than the Advisor, she looked much older. "Such a charming woman," she thought to herself. The last time she saw her she had graciously called to her from across the room "Lady! You look splendid! How slender you've gotten," she had given her usual handkerchief wave back. She always carried a chiffon scarf in her hand. It came in handy for so many necessities. They were weaving their way through the 300 or so bamboo chairs at the annual all class high school reunion. It was always held at the local catering hall, resplendent in green velvet décor. Lady was always seated next to her steady stand in boyfriend Mickey. A beautiful man who was the son of the Chief of the Fire department and whom she would have married yesterday if he would have asked her. She knew he never would. He was local royalty, he was another first son of an ancient family in Sicktowne. She knew his plan. He was being patient, carefully choosing his wife from the graduating Senior high girls. He felt that he was finally ready to settle down. Running with the local ladies was getting him nowhere. Time for a fresh new Philly! He wasn't a womanizer, he was just bored by this hole-in-the-wall dump of a town. No matter how much they tried to build it up, it was rotten at the core and everybody knew it. "Stinkin'Sicktowne," she giggled to herself. They'd *never* get the stink off of it. This year the daughter of the owner of the largest car dealership had invited him to her "coming out" party. An unusual event for this area, the debutantes Mother was Southern and apparently that's how they did things "down there." He was all for it. He was going to pour on the charm and win her! Finally, a female who gave him a challenge. "These young ones" he'd told her one afternoon in his office, "they know they've got the world on a string!" He wished he'd figured that out 25 years ago. It wasn't a bad life, it was just getting to be too predictable. Time to jazz things up. Her purse wasn't too shabby either. He knew the dealership raked in at least a billion dollars a year. He already had everything he could want but a bigger house at Davis Park, Fire Island was always something to hope for. He was planning to call this next one "Sea Paradise." Lady blew the Advisors wife an air kiss and responded, "always a pleasure Tessa!" The room was buzzing and settling down but the exchange between Lady and Tessa turned everyone's head in their direction. "She knows," thought Lady, "everybody does." She was glad to feel Mickey's beautiful bicep as he stood up and stepped into a peck on her cheek. "That's as close as I'll ever get to a real kiss from you Mickey!" she giggled. He was turned on by the tight fitting apple butter yellow chiffon pantsuit she had strutted into the room wearing. "Oh, really!" he guffawed. He put his right hand behind the small of her back and his other behind her head and right there in the middle of the room he dipped her and gave her the warmest, wettest kiss he could deliver. The tables around them started to applaud and for the first since she was 5, he saw her blush. "That was last season," Lady remembered. Another year older and nothing promising on the horizon. At least she had her daughter and her young future to look forward to, and now she felt the even she was being taken away from her. She needed something to pull her forward. The past was always going to be a dead shell. She was deciding which dress to wear for a late night dinner with the Advisor. He loved the cornflower blue on her but tonight she felt like wearing black.

She had color coordinated her wardrobe lightest to darkest in her closet so she was thumbing through the blues and purples, down to the blacks. The black was sometimes harsh looking on her Mother of Pearl skin tone. With her long blonde hair and hazel brown eyes, she was still beautiful as she approached 45. She chose the black dress with eyelash lace on the bodice. She knew the Advisor would love the satin skirt. It reminded him of seeing her in lingerie.

Chapter 5

"This is my Manhattan"

Dinner with Lady was an experience like none
other. Each time he was with her it affected the
Advisor like a mini vacation. All his cares fell
away when he saw her. She smelled like
Magnolias and sunshine. He had planned to have a
little fun with her before dinner but the meeting
with the "Thug Union" at the bar had run long.
He'd have to settle for some deep kisses and
cuddles. He knew she'd give him a struggle
because she would already made up and dressed
when he arrived. He'd try anyway, he would
always try to get closer to Lady. He felt like a King
with her on his arm and people responded! For a
short hot minute he was able to shed his country
boy roots and be the Mogul that he was about
become. Once the Linen Building was completed
he would have more than enough money to get and
give Lady everything she deserved. Tonight they

were dining with his best friend from the Art world. A man who had earned his reputation by building sculptures in his back yard. The Advisor had been invited to a barbecue at the Sculptors house one afternoon and he stopped to marvel at the carved wooden stabiles. The work was mediocre, but the friendship was outstanding. That was the story of how he met "Arty." The two of them grew to be the planners of the new "Sicktowne." He hated that ever since Lady had told him her name for his town he couldn't get it out of his head. He felt the same way she did but he wasn't allowed to admit it. He had to keep on working with the same old crowd that he had engaged for the past 20 years or he'd be just another bag in the Great South Bay. Lady had an idea about his arrangements but he couldn't tell her everything or she'd be in the bag with him. They were meeting Arty at a Manhattan club about 90 minutes away depending on the traffic. The 60 miles would give him plenty of time to loosen her up with alcohol and to put them both in the loose and free mood that the Artists enjoyed. The uptight suburban mindset did not play well in the Manhattan Art scene. This was his last meeting with the group of Artists that he was regularly "transplanting,' one by one into his Art House. It was critical to the town plan that he populate the area with as many Manhattan Artists as he could. The Linen Building was specifically designed as a resort for the wealthiest Art Collectors from Manhattan and he was excited to be closing the deals. Last time in he had told the crowd about how grateful he was to invite them to his town, they had cheered when he said "This is My Manhattan." They were excited to get "cheap" rent and still be able to ride in on the train for the 50 minute ride back "to Town." Every snob in Manhattan referred to the city as "Town." The Advisor knew he was no city slicker, and he was proud to proclaim his birthplace. It was fun to step off of "the Island" and rub elbows with the sophisticates. He could see the effect that the new blood had on the people in his town. It seemed like "out with the old and in with the new" was the mindset now. Sicktowne had been ill for the past 30 years and because of his efforts, it wasn't sick anymore. It was thriving. Everyone was amazed at the turn around, they marveled as if it was an accident, they'd meet him at the local coffee shop and say "It was bound to happen sooner or later!" There was no accident here, this took vision and determination. The Bumpkins couldn't fathom the big picture until he brought it to them. Ironically, his plan was to build it and leave it right where he found it. His life with Lady would take place on a different, warmer shore. That's what he was thinking as he pulled up to her tiny house, just North of town in the Kingdom Lake section, North of town—the drug capital of Sicktowne. Full of addicts and alcoholics he noted as he glanced up at the loose sneakers hanging by their shoe laces off of the street wires. The entire development was underwater and he knew most of them were going to be kicked out soon. A "house cleaning," the area was still "quiet" but a builder had just plunked down 5 million dollars to develop the North side of the lake and the houses would be worth much more after that. Better to get the deadbeats out now, take the houses in foreclosure save a buck. Lady had grown up here. He was surprised that she chose to come back. The tiny house suited her though. She felt compassion for the area, she knew that many of the original owners were Vietnam Veterans like her older Brother. Like a lot of people she was still angry about the treatment that her Brother and all the Vietnam Veterans received when he came home. She had told him of a time when she was excited and proud to go to the local mall with her big Brother, he hadn't been home from Vietnam a month and he was still wearing his Army uniform with her to the mall. He was tense as he walked through the crowded area. As they approached a sunken seating area a group of filthy long haired "Hippies" came around the corner. The war in Vietnam was raging and the war at home to end the war was raging. They eyed her Brother with hatred. One of them spit on her Brothers beautiful uniform. Her Brother restrained himself from pummeling the Hippie to death. They left the mall and he never wore the uniform again. She never discussed or watched anything that had to do with the Vietnam War. She knew that if this area ever needed a street Army those Vietnam Vets would be the first ones to jump in. It didn't matter how old they got either, they were "all warriors till the day they die," she always told him. It was a taboo subject around her. The only other group she had any respect for were the Marines. She loved their code of honor and their sense of duty. She had never had a problem at her house (until now?) he remembered her telling him that she thought her neighbors were trying to follow her. Even if she did he knew she would never call the local Police, she would only deal with the Sheriffs Office because she said "they don't stink of the Sicktowne corruption on them." She had asked him to help the area come up. He couldn't do anything for her, it was out of his hands. The Linen Building only had about 68 low income units. He was saving them for the local relatives of his Trustees. He pulled his collar close as he rushed to the door in the chilly late Fall air. The night was clear and crisp and as he opened her screen door he could smell her before he saw her. "Everything about her is sweet," he thought as he felt for the key. He pushed in and warmed his hands under his armpits as he moved across the tiny shabby chic living room towards her bedroom in the back of the house. It only took 3 steps to cross the room and he caught a glimpse of her at her dressing table applying a bit of perfume to her neck. "I love her," he was surprised to think. He had a small blue velvet box in his pocket and he produced it behind her head, the reflection in the mirror caught her eye. "Oh honey, you're adorable!" she purred.

That was all he needed to hear. He slid his hands onto her shoulders and downward to place the box in the palm of her right hand. He was busy nestling his mouth into her warm fleshy shoulder as she popped open the box and giggled at the diamond and gold bracelet inside. "The XO pattern is for the kisses and hugs I'm expecting this evening," he whispered as he nibbled on her earlobe. She turned easily in the silk skirt and swung her legs around on the small tufted bench so he could bend to kiss her. After a few minutes she stood up and held out her left arm, "Please dear, put it on me, I can't wait to see it sparkle." He took the box and slid the bracelet down her arm to clasp it at her wrist. "How did you know that my wrist was so tiny!" She remarked. "I know everything about you," he replied as he pulled her close to him for more cuddling. She sighed, "We'll have to be going if we want to arrive on time," she said in a sing-song voice. "I know," he said, "I know." He pressed his lips to her one last time and stepped away like a kid from sticky candy. "Let me clean up for a minute and we'll get going." I got a text from my driver, the Limo is waiting out front." He headed toward the tiny bathroom and she took his coat to the living room. Her charcoal grey faux fur wrap was on the back of the sofa and she gathered up her purse and took a quick sip of her drink, a stale rye and ginger ale. He finished it for her and they headed out the front door.

Chapter 6

The Linen Building

The crown jewel in Sicktowne was the newly constructed "Linen Building." A six story apartment complex designed with a resort style feel. It was key to creating an Artistic Empire in the town. The "Art House" went up last year and it was the first new building to be built in the town in 30 years. It only held 35 affordable housing units and it was full within 6 months. The local kids were the first to come in and now, 2 years later they had moved out almost every single one of them. It wasn't that they didn't have any talent, it was that each apartment was more valuable when it housed a Manhattan Artist. Over the course of the last year the management applied a new lighting bill fee and a heating bill fee on the local kids. It worked like a charm and that was enough to push most of the Bumpkins right out the door. The Manhattan Artists were being moved in to provide a million dollar industry to the Wall Street crowd that was being moved into the Linen Building. It's a standard formula, lift up an impoverished area with Artists, grow it, let it build to become an "Artists colony," drive the price of real estate in the area sky high. Move the starving Artists out and triple the rents. It worked all over Manhattan and it was going to work here. It wasn't easy to push it through the local community, they resisted the modern appearance and rejected the thought of crazy unwashed Artists wandering around the town. He pushed for it and it took a couple of years to get community support. In the end, the Advisor was going to be filthy rich and that was all he cared about. The Linen building was almost completely sold out. 230 units were ready to become his fortune. He had made good Manhattan connections and he was able to barter a deal for himself for a beautiful Manhattan Penthouse and he wanted to move Lady into it as soon as possible. He was planning to invite her to view it tonight after his meeting with the Manhattan Artists. He was going to use it as a jumping off point for their Winter homes in the South. He had asked the designers to copy the style she was used to at her home in Kingdom Lake. He had taken the time to photograph the small house and bring them the ideas for designing the Penthouse to please Lady. He was planning to spend the weekend there with her. They could act like newlyweds! The traffic was moving and Lady was delightful. She filled his head with dreams of a stress free and lighthearted future. A balm to his battered soul. The push to build and keep the "big money boys" happy had been taking a toll on him and he was weary of the chase. "Thank God I've had Lady by my side through all of this! I can't imagine what would be left of me if she hadn't come along." Lady was on her third whiskey and she was really beginning to come out of her shell. "Look babe! The lights! It's almost as beautiful as my new sparkle!" Lady referred to all her jewelry as "sparkle." Over the past 6 years he had given her almost $20 thousand dollars worth of jewelry—his Jeweler gave him the total with each new thing he ordered for her. He didn't bother to keep track of how much he spent for her clothes, all he cared about was that she always looked beautiful and he always told her "If you want it Sweetie, just point your finger and we'll get it." He wanted her to be happy. They pulled up to the store front, double parked and watched to see who had already arrived. The party was in full swing. They could see Arty pinned into a corner with a scantily clad 20 something sucking up to him. His face had the delighted look he always wore when he was luring a "young tidbit" into his bed. "Arty's in his Heaven, the Advisor called out to Lady. She was readjusting her garments that had run askew of the Advisors hands on the 75 minute drive in, they had made good time. She started to giggle and slipped on her silver shoes. The Advisor pushed open the door and reminded his driver to be back in 2 hours. He was starving and the hors d'oeuvres wouldn't be enough to hold him until dinner. Lady was always hungry and the whiskey made her delicious so he would have to load her up with the finger food to keep her going. Dinner was at Carmines and then off to the new Penthouse. They climbed out and could see Arty waving through the window. He had gathered a group of Artists around the entrance to greet them as they came in. The Advisor took a deep breath and pulled the door open for Lady as she wobbled past him, the booze was hitting her full force. Once she stepped in the door most of the attention went to her and he was free to step aside with Arty. "Hey buddy! How ya been?" Arty called out. "I'm all right guy, how's things going?" the Advisor replied. "We've got it all covered now and everyone is going into the Art House by the end of the month. I heard from one of the Realtors and she said she signed the last owner for the Linen Building yesterday. It was some kind of project huh?" "Yep," the

Advisor agreed, "we finally put it to bed, we
finally did it." Both men had grabbed a cup of
white wine as the server made his way over. Both
men clicked their cups and drank down the golden
liquid. "Swill!" the Advisor shot out to Arty as he
swallowed the warm liquid. Arty's eyes bulged
and he laughed out loud. Lady was working the
crowd with the group who had come to the door,
"She's on fire tonight, a real fire cracker," thought
the Advisor. At these events she was like water in
the desert, he was so worn down from his weekly
hustle that he loved to stand back and watch
someone else shine. Arty had moved off to woo his
young thing and the Advisor finally had a minute
to himself. He wasn't working this crowd, he knew
he wasn't one of them. Lady was always the center
of attention, all of the Artists moving into the Art
House were men. Gay or straight, they love her.

Chapter 7

The party, dinner and to the Penthouse at last. The
Advisor was exhausted. Lady was too. Her head on
his shoulder felt just right as the driver wound
through the city streets over to the building. Lady
wasn't paying any attention, she thought they were
heading home. She was settling in for the long
drive. The car stopped and the Advisor nudged her
gently and quietly said "Surprise." She looked out
the window at the beautiful double doors that led
to the lobby. "What is this?" she asked sleepily.
"It's our new home." he replied. "Let's go in." The
driver had instructions to sleep late and the
Advisor led Lady through the luxurious lobby
towards the elevator. The night shift security guard
was already acquainted with him from the times he
had arranged to let the decorators in. He gave him
a nod and they headed up. Lady eyes were wide
open as she adjusted to the lighting. She wrapped
her arms around his neck and kissed him until the

elevator stopped at the top floor. "You are incredible," she repeated over and over again. The elevator opened and she gave out a "small yelp" she saw that the room suited her taste and was a larger more lavish version of her own living room. "Darling, it's just like home!" She was giddy as a little girl as she flitted from sofa to table to lamp. "This IS a surprise!" The joy in her face lit up the room for him and he felt peaceful for the first time in years. Arm in arm they moved towards the floor to ceiling windows to inhale the stupendous view of the city, the lights twinkled to the beat of their hearts. The Advisor was fading with fatigue and he knew Lady was too so he said "Let's take a walk to the bedroom." Lady kept pace with him as he opened the door to the master suite. Champagne colored lights made the room glow golden. Even the satin spread on the bed was the color of Champagne. The accent color was rose gold. For him, the designer had added brown burgundy bedroom furniture. For her, the drapes were Ivory satin with oversized fluffy cotton candy pink flowers, the trim was brown burgundy. The carpet was white ivory to match the drapes. Brushed nickel hardware and lamps made the room flicker in the soothing light. Lady and the Advisor, from years of routine began to undress. They crawled into the King sized bed and met in the middle. He was on his back and she was resting her head on his shoulder. Silently and immediately they fell asleep. In the early morning hours, the Advisor was moving slowly through the rooms of the apartment. He marveled at how the decorators had followed his every request. The apartment gave him what he wanted, the feeling of being on vacation. He was looking forward to many hours of peace with Lady in this place. The large living room done in shades of grey and terracotta felt beach like to him. The subtle sky blue accents kept it light hearted. He was at the door now, looking for the newspaper. The foyer was dimly lit and the French blue coating was a heavy contrast from the grey, white and terracotta lightness of the Penthouse. The newspaper was there along with a rolling dolly cart that was filled with everything necessary for a continental breakfast. "The doorman really came through" he thought. Hot coffee and lots of it is what he needed to get his vim and vigor going. Lady loved her milky tea. "Perfect," he said to himself. He rolled the cart into the bedroom and created his "cup of morning" as Lady called it. Black and sweet was how he liked it. No news in the paper to speak of, and Lady began to rouse at the smell of the coffee. "Hi honey," she called over to him from across the bed. He gave her his morning smile and waited for her to wake up before he moved over to spoon with her. "Happy dear?" he asked her gently, "very happy dear," she replied. "I hope we can spend our lives together here my love," he began, "my dream is to get away from Sicktowne forever. I'll be out of a job in 3 years and I am ready for it. I want you to come with me. I've finished up all the legwork for the Linen Building and the Art House is taking off as planned. They won't need me or miss me around there anymore. I have put away enough money to keep us happy for the rest of our lives and Tessa wants out. Do you think we can do this together?" Lady was warm and cozy and slightly fuzzy from the alcohol she had from the night before. Listening to her soft steady breathing was hypnotic to him and her body was so comfortable to his. "My beautiful body pillow," he thought out loud." Lady giggled and said "Sweetie, I don't know what to do now, I have my daughter to think of too and you're forgetting about the new building going up in the Spring, you call it your "money machine" or something like that. When do you want to cut your ties and start living here?" The Advisor was disconcerted, he wasn't expecting Lady to be looking into the details this morning. He wanted it to be a slow and sweet morning and he was annoyed that she couldn't just say "yes" to everything he was suggesting. "Let's not dwell on the details right now honey," he sighed, "let's just enjoy the dream for this morning—ok?" She heard the small annoyance in his voice and realized that he was holding out his heart to her. She knew she could never commit to the Penthouse full time. He was trying to lock her away in the tower and it was a beautiful tower, but still, it was a tower. He had 15 years on her and he wasn't getting any younger. She had seen it happen to so many of her friends who married older men. The guys just didn't hold up. They had all good intentions at the start for a "new life full of travel and activity." 3 years in they start to fizzle out and the lady is left like a "Nurse with a Purse" to take care of them. She was not going to spend her 50's playing Mother to an aging crank. The Advisor was drifting off to sleep and she startled him by asking "Tell me about the "Money Maker," she remembered it was going to be called "The Majestic Club." It was tied into the Art House and the Linen Building somehow. The money was just being pushed around between the buildings in Sicktowne. There was only a hand full of people who controlled the money and the Advisor was one of them. She was trying to figure out a way to make some money herself. Oh, he was all right and she lived carefully on the $40 thousand dollars that he gave her every year but why shouldn't she have a chance to invest in something that would pay off and give her some financial freedom from him? She knew a lot more than she let on after spending many nights pouring over the contents of the Advisors briefcase after he'd fallen asleep in her bed. She had been speaking to Mickey about it for the past 16 months and he was helping her develop her own plan for the future. The Advisor mumbled, "Maybe later," and drifted back to sleep.

Chapter 8

Mickey takes a wife

He was sliding his slippers onto his soggy feet
when the telephone rang by his bed. He picked it
up and said "hello," it was Lady. "Are you heading
over to the reception, handsome?" she asked. "I'm
getting ready to go" he replied. "I hope you have a
lot of fun over there, you'll be the most eligible
Bachelor in the room!" He gave a laugh and said
"My dear, that was so ten years ago." She knew it
was true but why dwell on the negative?
"Nonsense Mr. Man, you can have any doll you
want from that crowd, so go get yourself the best
one." "That is my intention," he responded. "I'll
give you a holler when I get back." "Love" she
said quietly and hung up. He was dry now after his
shower and the black pants and white shirt stared
at him, naked, from the closet. GQ Crisp was the
look he was going for and he had even purchased a
new suit, cut to flatter his figure like the young

men were wearing nowadays. Not like the baggy things he was used to wearing that looked like his Fathers clothes. "Fashion keeps you young," is what Lady always said and the girl he wanted was just that—young. He finished putting on his jacket, slipped on his Italian black leather loafers and headed down the elevator to the ground floor. His black Buggatti was waiting, angle parked into the 2 spots reserved for his apartment. He was the first resident of the brand new Linen Building. He slid into the sleek machine and listened to it purr. He loved it because it was everything his Father wasn't. He was tired of the 'back woods mentality' that his Father was stuck in and he would never go back to driving a refurbished Ford pickup. That was his High School memory. This engine represented the man that he had become. Chicks loved it too and that didn't hurt. He had seen his share of 'em. Now he really wanted to settle down with a wife and invest in a family car. The Buggatti would be his for nights out with the guys.

A chance to revisit his youth. "By this time next year, I'll be heading over for dinner at the Country Club with my bride," he was thinking as he put the car in reverse. "I hope she learns to cook, that would really please Mother." He was lost in his thoughts as he pulled right onto Old Monte Avenue then another quick left at the white clock on Jane to travel the 6 or so blocks to the catering hall. Sicktowne was bustling and getting ready for another drunken Saturday night festival. He laughed to himself as he remembered Lady calling it "Vomit Night in Sicktowne," because when the bars closed down the crowds would wander the streets vomiting on the sidewalks, planters, store fronts--everywhere. By the light of day, the streets were busy with shoppers, after dark the dinner crowd came through, then the bar crowd followed. The Advisor had brought in 10 more bars and restaurants over the past 2 years and the business owners were bearing the brunt in property damages. If they weren't puking on it, they were destroying it. He continued past the rows of stores he had seen his whole life, stopping to let a small group cross at the crosswalk in front of the Library. The black community clock let him know he was going to be late. He was moving quickly down Jane Street, past the Post Office, through the intersection at "Accident Alley" and he saw his "childhood playground" on the right. "The Black Wood Bar," he had played in as a child with a friend whose Father owned it. He remembered hours of shuffleboard with the town drunks, they weren't bad guys. His friends Mother was a real beauty who was tricked into divorcing his Father by the town swindler, he recalled. The guy thought she had lots of money and he set out to get it. She didn't and he left, but not before giving her a daughter to remember him by. Not an unusual occurrence in Sicktowne. The crooks were very creative, the Politicians even more so. He was at the catering hall on the left and "I'm not very late after all," he thought. He could see the High

School girls trickling in wearing their most daring dresses. To be 18 again! He remembered it well, sweet Summer nights and fun. His best friend spent one whole Summer with him rebuilding the engine of his old Ford pick-up truck and that year-- he had a bed in the "bed." He rarely saw any of his old girlfriends now, most had moved away. Only Lady was still around, so beautiful and so lonely. He had begun to feel the same way lately and he was hoping that a young bride would bring back the feeling of his glory days. "You don't get too many new chances or new beginnings as the years go by," he mused. As he walked to the door he paused to enjoy the new fountain, a great photo spot for the wedding crowd. It was bigger than he remembered and at night it was lit up for a beautiful romantic effect. He had no intention of getting married here, it wasn't in the right place, he would never have anything to do with the merchants in Sicktowne, he knew better. "There are a lot of unsavory characters in Sicktowne," he could hear Lady saying. She knew as much as he did about the place, if not more. He heard his name, "Mickey!' he was on line to meet his future Mother-in-law, Lola. She was warm and charming and he hoped her daughter would be the same way. She grabbed his face with both hands and kissed him on both cheeks. "Emerald will be thrilled to see you! Go on in, your table is marked. Don't forget to say hi to Emeralds Daddy, he's holding court inside near the bar." He made his way across the crowded room, waving here and there as he saw a friend, business acquaintance or cousin. The usual local crowd was in attendance. No one would say no to Red. His car dealership was holding up the town and pretty much everyone who owned a car bought it at "Red Cars Auto Dealership." 85 years was all the history he needed and his company records held the financial history of just about every household in the town. He could have been Mayor, but the job wasn't worth the hassle. The pay was chump change to him. He was running the town his own way anyhow, he didn't need an Advisor or a board of Trustees to get in his way. Mickey was interested in knowing what he did with that billion dollar paycheck every year. Where was he putting that money? The buildings seemed to be going up faster and faster each year and he had a hunch that Red was the man who was generating that construction. He wanted "in" on it and marrying Emerald would put him in a good spot he thought. Lady wanted some money and he planned to help her feather her own nest somehow. He wasn't going to forget about one of his oldest friends. He saw Emerald at the candy bar and blew her a kiss. She looked so young surrounded by her cheerleader friends. She was pretty, not beautiful, she was still small the way High School girls can be—slender because they weren't all "filled out" yet. She was clever but not as intelligent as he was and he liked it that way. Lady was the only woman who could ever keep up with him. She was sharp; Emerald was too but her youth didn't afford her the experience that Lady had. No worries, he'd be just fine in that marriage. Even if he bored her, he'd keep her interested long enough to get a couple of kids out of her and he'd settle into middle age quite happily. Red was waving for him so he passed on the civilities at the tables and headed straight towards the bar. He elbowed his way into the circle of cronies that were vying for Reds attention. His outstretched hand met Reds huge size 11 and he felt like a boy with a giant. He always felt that way around Red. "How's it goin' Mickey," he smiled. "It's all good Red, no problems, Emerald looks beautiful so that makes it all worth it right?" Red beamed at him and agreed, "she is a looker, my baby girl, a real sweet girl." Mickey leaned closer and added, "I'm looking for a sweet girl Red, got any ideas?" Mickey could see the surprise flash across Reds face. "You're here alone my boy? You lookin' to settle down now are ya Mickey?" he asked. "I'm lookin'" Mickey nodded and he turned his head and gave another nod with his chin pointing towards Emerald. "Now *that* is a proposition that I might like to consider." Red answered. "We're having an 'after party' at the house tonight around 8pm, make yourself available and you can fight it out with about a dozen others, we'll see who keeps her fixated." Red was turning to address the waiter who was over his left shoulder indicating that it was time for photographs. He waved to Mickey and walked towards the fountain. "Wonder why he held this shindig in this place?" Mickey thought to himself. Probably the hot spot for the kids at the High School, they don't like to spend their money out of town. Sends a message to the other merchants too. High School keeps them loyal to the town for a while. Emerald could have done way better, she could have had anything she wanted. "I bet there will be every kind of happiness money can buy at that mansion tonight, he thought to himself as he found his table. He was sitting just across from the lead table, a perfect view of Emerald. He was excited to be invited and he sat next to one of the salesmen from Reds Auto dealership. His family had started out just one town over and had moved the dealership to Sicktowne 20 years ago. He had a dealership on the North and South end of "accident alley." A car rental dealership in the middle made it easy to make money off of the trade in's that he couldn't sell. He had a chain link fence company that fenced everything in, on his properties and on all the schools in the district. He had other businesses, one of the restaurants in town, a hair salon, and more he knew, but what they were he wasn't sure. One of the car lots was right around the corner from where he was sitting. He wondered if Red owned this place too. He wouldn't be surprised. He went back to the bar to order a beer. "Anything stronger and I'll be loopy by 8pm" he thought. He hated feeling nervous around *any* female. He shouldn't be, he knew, but this was the big catch and he really didn't want to blow it. His cool charade fell away whenever he tried to banter with Emerald. She was so young that she thought the world was as simple as her life. The lights were dimming for her entrance into the room with Red and everyone was looking towards the doors now. There she was, coming in like a bride, Mom on one side, Dad on the other. Everyone cheered, her High school friends whooped and whistled and as she passed, she looked at him as if she knew his secret. "Oh hell, Red spilled the beans," he realized. Keeping her attention was going to be much more difficult now. Red knew what he was doing, he was gonna make Mickey *work* for it. "I got no game with her now," he groused under his breath. He'd have to make things interesting, pull out all the stops.

Chapter 9

Lady

Lady was mopping at her face as she watched her
daughter drive away. She was shaken to the core
by the exchange she was just a victim of. Her
daughter had been changing over the past year and
things were getting worse by the day. It finally
stopped and revealed itself as her daughter created
an argument with her and left. The thought of
never seeing her daughter again made her sick in a
way she had never felt before. Her daughter was as
cool as a cucumber as she cored out Lady's heart.
"She's like her Father" she thought to herself and
she realized that the message she just received
came straight from him. "That bastard!" She
hadn't seen him or heard from him in years. Now,
as her daughter had become Lady's best friend,
that bastard tore her away from her. She slowly
closed her front door and slumped onto the couch.
That was her baby! She was going to miss out on

all the beautiful events in the coming out years now. She wondered if the gang of thugs who were following her had something to do with it. She had heard her daughter complain over the past year about being followed herself. Last year her daughter had said "They're following you too, you just don't know about it yet." She pieced together the events of the past year as her daughter told them to her. They were hard to believe. Now that the same thing was happening to her, she felt a pain and remorse for watching her daughter go through it alone. It broke her heart. The hunting party that was following her drove her daughter out of the house. Her daughter was so terrified of being home that she made a fight with her Mother to run away with her new boyfriend. Lady felt the knot in her stomach tighten. Against her better judgment she had gone to the local Police precinct, to Police Headquarters, to the District Attorneys office, and to the FBI. No one would help her, she wasn't surprised. That's how things were done in

Sicktowne. She was afraid to tell the Advisor, he was her last friend. Everyone else had been driven away from her and she didn't know why. They just stopped returning her phone calls one day. Her Lawyer, her therapist, and the service personnel she had used for years all used the same formula, creating a made up argument so they could tell her not to call anymore, "My office can't help you, find someone else," they all said. Nobody wanted to know her anymore. "Who had put this "hit" out on her," she wondered. She had been wondering about it for the past 8 months. A clue came when an old Lawyer friend said "Ever since I met you I gotta pay 3x the amount as everyone else to have any repairs done to my home." What the heck did that mean?" She knew she was being followed by her neighbors, she knew she was living 6 blocks from the local Home Dispatch store. What was the connection? Her house was tiny, she had only 4 windows. Lately, everywhere she went in her car found her to be surrounded by 4x4 trucks.

Everywhere. She thought, 4 windows, all measured 44"x44", was that the connection? She never remembered her ex-husband having anything to do with the construction business. The last time they had gone to a party was something like 10 years ago, it was a party for a popular television show that swooped into a neighborhood and refurbished the house of a needy hero "for free." The television show had the power to get the local town offices to push through all the permits needed to make the project run smoothly. Her ex-husband worked with all the county people who controlled those permits. Lady knew that the company that did the construction was all "Thug" run. She remembered feeling oddly afraid as she watched the couples in the restaurant celebrate. The party was a celebration for all the workers and their wives who had made the project ready to air for the scheduled television time slot. Something else was going on that evening too and she had heard whisperings that it was like some sort of round up of people who had houses that needed work. The house that she had lived in with her ex-husband needed windows too. It had 4 old windows across the front that measured 44"x44", just like this one. She had seen the 4x4 trucks driving past the house daily now that she thought about it. She had gotten the same cold shoulder from the neighbors there too. She didn't become a shut in because she sold the house and moved before they could do it to her. This time she hadn't seen it coming. She'd been trapped. She had bought the house on the dead end street thinking it would be safer. She never realized until this year that it would just make it easier to know when she was coming in and out of the block. It only took one homebound neighbor to keep track of her schedule and there were plenty of men and women out of work on her block. Sitting home with nothing to do all day. She had seen her neighbor out with a clipboard, keeping track of her schedule as she went by. Behind her house she could open her patio door and see 10 houses with windows and doors all facing her house, all were part of the neighborhood group that was now surveilling her. They kept in constant contact through a free cell phone service. It had taken her months of observation and investigation to discover their methods. They had watched her house for 8 years, they knew she had no family besides her daughter, a handful of friends and besides the Advisor, not many visitors to her home. They never followed her when the Advisor could see and that was the plan, to make her out to be crazy. Now the only time she left the house was to go out with the Advisor. Nobody ever followed her when she was with him. Her days used to be filled with friends and lunches and shopping. Now she stayed home, pacing around in her tiny, remodeled cabin. She had lived there for the past 8 years and after her awful neighbor experience at the last house, she never bothered to get to know her neighbors here. Yet they were following her whenever she left the house, she was sure of it. The only other event that took place there and here was the car accident. Both times she was stopped in traffic and hit in the rear by a speeding car. This time her daughter was with her. She was still waiting to settle the lawsuit and her Lawyer was stalling for some reason. She had been calling the desk Sargent at the local Precinct for months to complain about being followed, the only thing they had to say was that it is legal to follow anyone who has an open auto insurance case. They weren't going to help because the guys who were following her were all off duty Detectives making a buck off of the auto insurance company who had legally hired them to legally follow her to disprove her claim for damages for her injuries. The accident had snapped her neck and she endured a spinal surgery. She recovered over the past year and she felt that she had to take her eye off of her daughter for that year and they were able to torment the child who had no other family to go to. Her phones were tapped and her email accounts were hacked. She knew they were able to look over all of her financial accounts. She wasn't sure who they were but as the months had gone by she was able to piece together a picture of a web of thugs all coming at her to destroy her life. She didn't want to tell the Advisor because she was afraid he might run away from her life too. She dragged herself over to her bed and wept herself to sleep. She woke up feeling dead inside and was surprised and nervous when she checked her cellphone and didn't have a message from the Advisor. The pattern was to make an argument with her and stop returning her phone calls. She knew that if the Advisor left her now she wouldn't be able to go on. She also knew that whoever was doing this to her wanted her to kill herself. She knew that if she didn't kill herself she would have to move and try to figure out a way to rebuild her life. She thought about the Penthouse and realized that the Advisor would leave her there like a trophy and she would have to create an entirely new life again. She wasn't up to the task, she did not want to try again without her daughter. Aging alone was not something anyone looks forward to. She still had Mickey and that was helping her hold on. She went to the kitchen to face her mail. Eight months ago her mortgage was sold to some investment group. She had asked who they were and all she could find out was that they were a group who was involved in the building industry. She had just found out that the investment group who bought her house was the financial institution that backed the credit cards for the Home dispatch store that was stalking her to buy new windows. Yesterday she found out that she was scammed by a company that pretended to be the holder of her mortgage. 8 months ago they had contacted her to refinance her mortgage. She agreed and they sent her paperwork through one of the speedy delivery services. She had faxed over every pertinent financial document that she had. They knew all about her life and her money and they were a fraudulent company located in the Midwest. She laughed to herself thinking that they probably thought she was loaded and she was flat broke. The only money missing was nine hundred dollars from a child support card. There wasn't anything else. She believed that once the Home dispatch store bought her mortgage, they had their fraudulent company contact her for the refinance documents to get at any money she might have saved. She had heard from friends who also had their homes in foreclosure and any one of them who had money in a savings account lost it when their mortgage bank froze the account and claimed the money for the debt owed on the mortgage. They didn't care how much or how little money they got. They just swooped in and took the money. After that they would get the neighbors involved to drive the people from their homes, and who would want to continue living in a neighborhood that was full of people that had turned on you anyway. Eight months ago she had started receiving large amounts of mail. She didn't have any bills to speak of and she was surprised by the increase in volume of the letters and advertisements. They all had non-profit or registered postmarks, nothing was ever stamped or postmarked through the local Post Office. She started to realize that a neighbor was probably dropping the fake mail into her box every day. The letters made no sense to her but she felt that they were trying to send her a message. She had carefully marked the date received on them and put each days mail into a zip lock baggie. She had bins full of them now. Over the course of the last 6 weeks she had begun to respond to the letters that were becoming imperative. False auto insurance information had made driving her car tricky. She had received mail saying her registration was revoked due to lack of insurance when she did have insurance and her registration was valid. She had responded to the letters to the offices that were located at the state capital because whenever she tried to resolve anything locally, it made matters worse. She knew she was being wounded to death. Every area of her life was being attacked and she was worn down as the months dragged on. Losing her daughter today made her feel utterly defeated. She understood why the girl had to run away, she was chased away and that made Lady furious. She was wounded by the false argument and she knew her daughter didn't want to do it, she knew her daughter had to save herself. Could it be that the Advisor was trying to get rid of her? It didn't fit in with the way he had acted last weekend at the Penthouse. He had made clear to her that he believed in a future with her. Was someone else trying to keep her "on ice" so she wouldn't be seen out in public with him? They were forcing her to stay in her house and the only thing she had to look at was the mail. Were they trying to get her attention? She looked over the mail. Today she got 5 advertisements for tax abatement. Someone was trying to tell her to grieve the taxes on her house to get them to be lowered. Her taxes were built into her mortgage and she hadn't paid her mortgage in 9 years. She couldn't afford it after her ex-husband had stopped giving her child support and alimony payments and she knew that in Sicktowne, the people who owned it would own it forever. They pushed out a fake mortgage, but they're just renting it out, making you think you're going to live in it and own it but you're really just going to die in it. He had powerful friends and there wasn't anything she could do about it. The Advisor had always asked her not to involve him in any of the activity that involved her ex-husband, he didn't want to deal with the bad press. Instead of dragging him back to a court that she knew she would never win in, she just stopped paying her mortgage. Once her daughter graduated from High School she had planned to leave the house anyway. She was done with the house now, but she wasn't being allowed to leave it! She could never release the wave of sickness that came over her whenever she let herself remember that she had no knowledge of where her daughter was at that very moment. "Where is she?" she would cry out in her mind. "Why can't I know about her life? What she is interested in, how she is getting through her day? The constant and overwhelming belief that her daughter had been forcibly removed from her home never left her. She churned with anger all day long. Nothing would keep her from exacting her revenge on Sicktowne, she knew everything there was to know about the sick machinations of the money machine down there. She just didn't know how to go about letting *other* people know. She knew it was the groups down town that were trying to hurt her by destroying her family. She had learned from her daughter that when you tell it to them like it's a story on television, they believe you but when you describe it as it is happening *to you* they call you crazy. The phone rang and she could see on the caller ID that it was Mickey. She decided to tell him. "Hi Mickey darling," she tried to sound cheerful as she answered the phone. Mickey was calling from his car as he drove over to Red's mansion for the after party. "I'm on my way," he sang into the phone. "How was the party?" she asked. "Fabulous!" he yodeled happily. She laughed and said "Are you on your way home, can you stop over?" He could hear a sadness in her voice, he wasn't sure why. "No doll, I'm heading over to the after party to wear down Emerald. Red gave me the go ahead and now I have to fight off the pack to make her mine," he chuckled sarcastically. "You okay?" he wondered. "Well, I just had a fight with my daughter and I'm out of my mind over it. I'm being followed everywhere I go and my neighbors are in on it too," she said matter of factly. " Oh my God" was all that Mickey could think of to say. "Are you all right?" he added. "No, not really, I'm a mess Mickey, a real mess. I don't know what to do. Have you ever heard of anything like this before?" "No, not really. It sounds bizarre. What the hell is going on up there in Kingdom Lake?" he asked. "This is coming from Sicktowne, there are too many moving parts to it to just be the neighborhood. When I bought this house, the old homeowner said something like this happened to her but I didn't put much stock into it. It sounded too crazy to believe. Now, it's a real thing and this group is mean Mickey. They hunted and stalked my daughter until she ran away. I haven't been able to leave the house for weeks now and I'm at my wits end. I haven't told the Advisor, he'd think I'm nuts! What am I gonna do" she burst into tears again. "Hey, Lady, calm down." Mickey stammered. He couldn't remember the last time he had heard Lady cry. "Just sit tight and I'll swing by tonight. I've got to go to this after party right now, okay?" he said softly. "Okay, Mickey, okay. Bye" Lady responded as she hung up the phone. She decided to lay down until Mickey came by. She was still crying as she dropped off to sleep. The house was pitch black as she opened her eyes to read the time on the neon clock on the cable box. 1 a.m. and no Mickey. She didn't care anymore. She didn't have anything or anyone left to care about. She decided to take a handful of pills that she had been saving for this day. She had stockpiled them in case she needed a "way out." Today she was getting out. The Advisor had never called her back and neither did Mickey. That was how it went over the past 8 months and she didn't want to endure the pain of knowing that they weren't ever going to call her again because there was nobody left that she knew. Her life had been completely extinguished by someone, for some reason she never discovered. The pills went down easy. She thought about all the women in Kingdom Lake who had killed themselves in their homes over the past 2 years. So many Mothers! It was the talk of the area. Always under the strangest of circumstance. Always Catholic women. She was enjoying a clear stream of consciousness for the first time in months. Perhaps because the pills enabled her to drop her guard. She had been to a Psychic 6 years ago who foretold of this day and these events and for months she had been remembering the bits and pieces of the Psychic reading as they came true. Every time she thought of it her head would spin because her mind was looking backwards and forwards at the same time. She was remembering what the Psychic said *would* happen, living through it *while* it was happening and anticipating what the Psychic said was *going* to happen. Her whole world had spun out of control and as she lay down on her bed she was glad to step out of the spin for the last time.

Chapter 10

Land of "Linen"

The months rolled by quickly as the "Thug Union" put the finishing touches on the Linen Building. They spent most of their days strolling in anytime around the 6am check-in and their afternoons playing street hockey, Bocci ball or throwing around a football in the underground garage. The Advisor didn't care, as long as he got his cut of their salaries, he was happy. There was only one tenant in the building when they got there and he was a "good ole' boy" like them. As long as they kept his Buggatti safe, he was happy. He would throw a ball around with them once in a while as he was heading out to his car. They saw him come out all Summer long wearing his linen suits and trousers, they started calling the building "The Land of Linen." They were on schedule through the Summer and new tenants were streaming in as the weather was turning into Autumn. Nobody had another job lined up and that was creating the same tension that it always did. Everyone knew the channel that they had to stay in to get more work. Another building was in the whisper mill and they were hungry for the job. They knew that when they saw the "Rainmaker," they could rest easy. He was a Trustee and he was the one who could pull the strings for them with the Building Inspection Department (BID.) The BID had the last word on every project. The Assessors office had the first. The "Rainmaker" worked for the Board of Elections. He was the one who got the guys into office who would pass all the permits through and give a building project the "Go." He was also on the board of the Peoples Art Covenant the Artists group that was pushing all the money into town from Manhattan. A lot of money was being funneled into town and the Thug Union wanted their fair share of it. The Linen Building was pushed through pretty quick and they wanted the next one, "The Majestic," a mega night club, to go

91

through for next season. They were irked by the interim project, an 1800's style building that was being refurbished further down on Main Street. They had missed their chance for that job because one of the guys in the Assessors Office wouldn't okay a berm for the basement. The Rainmaker took care of it. The rumor mill was full of gossip over the Spring and Summer and the guy finally caved in and gave his approval, just last week. The job went to another crew because the Thug Union already had work at the Linen Building. The Rainmaker had a sure fire formula that worked every time on guys who wouldn't play by the Thug rules. He called it "Face in the Crowd," just like the movie where the guy goes crazy in the end. Because whoever he did it to usually did end up crazy and sometimes they solved everybody's problems and killed themselves. He would have her group scout out a guys (or his girlfriends) house, watch the family, see their friends and relatives. He would have everyone followed everywhere they went. It was easy, he'd have his staff set up a website for a check in and a photo of the "Mark" and his family. They would post updates weekly. He would have every construction crew, highway crew, wiring company, water company and anyone else he wanted link on a free cellphone channel. He would get the Department of Labor building in town on it and move one of his kids into a job at the local dump coffee shop that was controlled by an older crowd of 20 somethings. The loser 20 somethings were stuck working there because of their addictions. Real losers, they called it the "Coffee Kup High School," because they came in to serve coffee, young at High School and left as burnt as a 40 year old—usually within 18 months. He'd start on the kid, usually a girl, when she was 15 or 16. Over the course of the next year, or for as long as it would take to break the guy, he would have the young girl brought into the circle of older workers. They would introduce her to the "wild fun" of booze, smokes, sex and eventually drugs if they could. They would monopolize all of her free time. They would ruin her school grades by keeping her out late, get her fighting with her parents. The Rainmaker would arrange for her school friends to invite her to all of their Sweet 16 parties. The parents would all be directly related to the project. Her parents would be driving her to and from the parties, so the Rainmakers technical group could get into the house and wire every inch of it. Phones, TV and computers, they would see and hear every conversation that went on in the house. They controlled the light switches, the appliances, the mail. They'd "blow up" the mailbox at the house with printed material from the local print shop. The mail carrier would pick up the fake mail on the way over to the guys house everyday. None of it had postmarks. They all used each others "registered mail" ID number and pass it around so they never paid for postage. They'd have the parents wading through fake mail, fake bills, fake insurance bills. The street mailboxes would be removed from the guys neighborhood. They'd run the parents back and forth to the Post Office. They'd make sure everyone saw the kid, everyone knew what she looked like. They'd take the photos from all the Sweet 16 parties and build a website that all the parents could check to start following her with. Like a "Most Wanted" page. Then they would "stage" a car accident on "accident alley" the road that was the main money maker for the crooked town Lawyers who were royalty through one of the ancient families. A little fender bender so she would have an open auto insurance case. The Rainmaker would get his local Art group membership to follow the kid, to gang stalk her, to terrorize her everywhere she went. If the parents went to the local Precinct, the crooked cops there would tell them it was legal to follow anyone who had an open auto accident. The parents would be steered over to the crooked Lawyer who owned the 50 feet of road on "accident alley" where the accident took place. Every Lawyer in town "owned" his or her share of 50 feet of "accident alley." Everybody shared the wealth. The Lawyer would stall the lawsuit for as long as it took to get the Father at the Assessors office to cave in on the project. The Coffee Kup workers would start to call her crazy whenever she mentioned being followed. They'd tell her "you must have hit your head in the accident." They would make fake arguments and turn away from her until every one of them was gone, she was friendless. She was turning 17. She was lost and overwhelmed. They would introduce a boy. The boy would become her world, slightly older than her, he would lure her out of her parents house. She would break her Fathers heart, make a false argument and go. The Father would be emotionally distraught at seeing his baby girl turned into a rubber doll. He'd blame it on the Mother, the Mother would blame it on the Father. What could he do? She's turning 18 in 6 months!! No court would touch it, no Lawyer would help him. The cops just laughed at him. He would be made to understand that she would be back just as soon as he passed the building project through. He gave in, the project pushed through. The boyfriend started fights with the girl, he asked her for rent money. He asked her for food money "You gotta contribute if you want to stay here." He turned cold on her. She couldn't go home, she knew she would be followed. The auto accident case would be settled by the crooked Lawyer. The girl would get a $300 dollar settlement. She would give it to the boyfriend. He'd laugh at her and throw her out. She would call her Mom and Dad and go back home, a wreck. The Rainmaker knew how to get things done. It worked just as well for the sons. This time there wasn't going to be a problem with the Majestic. They would make sure of that. The Rainmakers partners at the Board of Elections were Mortgage Bankers. They could float a loan or a bond, whatever would work for the project. Everything would pass through the local tax preparers office, the guy has a local following, he has been a Pastor at the local Church for the past 30 years. He hands it back over to the Trustee Rainmaker, and he does a walk through at a site that's being finished. If the guys see him, they know he's bringing them another job. The cycle of life continues in "Sicktowne."

Chapter 11

The Mayor

"Here comes the Fall again," the Advisor found himself thinking. He knew he would have to plan another meeting with the Thug Union. The Linen Building was done and they would be able to get by driving the oil trucks again this season, but Spring would be hell if he couldn't get the Majestic project going. The Mayors term would be up next January and he was glad to be able to plan his getaway. "This is my last season of this kind of garbage," he muttered to himself. He was checking his calendar to arrange another "boiler maker meeting" at the local steak house. "Monday night, don't forget to plan it for a Monday night," he repeated to himself as he scanned his schedule for the next month. He was horrified as his Secretary tapped lightly as his door and stepped into the room waving her cell phone. She handed him the text, he read them and looked up at her astonished face. He repeated the words he read and hoped he would never hear, the text said, "THEY WANT YOU TO RUN FOR MAYOR." He dropped into his chair, his Secretary took back her phone and sat on the small sofa across from his desk. "Oh my God," was all she said. He stared back at her for a few moments. They were both worked past their capacity everyday already so the job was not going to be a problem because he was already doing it. They were both planning on retirement after next year and that was the whole plan period. To turn their whole lives around now would be exhausting. They were silent as the wind blew the leaves through the trees outside his window. His first thought was for Lady, "I've got to talk to her." His next thought was for his wife, "She'll never go for it," he thought. His Secretary set him straight when she said, "You know you can't say no. It might not be so bad! You just gotta get the right Advisor and it'll be a cake walk. Hand over your office to the Advisor and become a figurehead just the way they always do it. You got no worries." she clamored. "Let me have a day to cope here," he responded. "Ask them, when do they want a face to face? and please bring me some coffee, I'm right in the middle of organizing a meeting for the new building, we'll work on the Mayor thing as it comes." The Secretary stood up and smiled, and said "Sure boss, no problem," she quietly closed the door behind her. "Damn," the Advisor pounded a fist on his desk. "I knew I'd never get out of this place!" He was furious and almost to the point of tears. He hadn't cried since his Mother died 18 years ago—what the hell!! "Settle down man," he soothed himself as he began to sway back and forth in his office chair. He spun slowly to look out the wide window. Trees blowing, colorful leaves changing and falling, everything was the same as it was 15 minutes ago when he was gleefully oblivious of his torturous future. Finally he let out a loud sigh, he hadn't realized he was holding his breath. "Let it go," he thought. "Acceptance is the answer to all my problems," he began to recite it in his head like a mantra. He thought about developing a health problem, creating a family emergency, causing a scandal. He thought about a lot of things but mostly he thought about his Penthouse dream for Lady and him. "It's not gonna happen the way I thought it would, but then it never does." He let himself mope and mourn for a few minutes alone. His Secretary tapped lightly again and set his coffee down on his blotter. She had a cup for herself and a pint of American whiskey. "We better drink while we can boss," she said as she poured half a shot into the coffee. They had been a team for the past 15 years and he was relieved to know she would be coming with him. "Make the phone calls Sam, make the phone calls. We're gonna need some support over here so you can start to organize and someone can fill in for you. The sooner we start, the better off we will be." They clicked their mugs together and swallowed. "We've got a great campaign slogan boss, she beamed, 'The Advisor is Wiser!' How do you like it?" He laughed and reminded her "We're already in office remember, we can't lose, they won't let that happen. It would cost them too much money." The office phone let out a chirp and she leaned over to pick it up, she listened and said "Please hold. It's Jack—"Jack of all trades," he's calling from the Linen Building work site. He says he wants to schedule a meeting with you. "Good, I was just planning that when you came in," he replied, "thanks for the juice." She nodded and left. He picked up and said "Hey Jack, I was just thinking of you." "Hi buddy, how are you doing?" Jack asked, he had heard the Mayor rumor. "I just want to let you know that I'm supporting everything you do and the boys and I are ready to go to work for you. I also want to say that I would be an excellent choice to fill in your shoes if that opportunity ever presented itself." The Advisor was not surprised, secrets traveled fast in Sicktowne. He was surprised to hear that Jack was looking to fill his spot. Jack was po' white trash. It would be hellish to get him into the group. He would do a great job but getting him in was not going to be easy. "I hear ya Jack," he replied and I appreciate what you're saying. I've heard from a few people already so I can't make any promises to you. You know I'm not the one to make that decision alone. If you circulate a little, see what you hear. Get back to me." "Will do," Jack answered. "I can schedule a 'Boiler maker' for the Monday after next if that's any help to you." "Great Jack, please do, I'm putting it on my calendar now and tell the boys that if they help me keep going, I'll have plenty of work for them, plenty of work," he hung up the phone. "At least I can Supervise the Majestic Building now, he thought. I was gonna have to keep on coming and going back and forth from the Penthouse to pick up my share of the money. Now, I can live in the best house in town until it gets built. He hadn't heard from Tessa yet, that was a good sign. That meant she wasn't throwing any kind of hissy fit. He hoped that her level head was on this morning, not her hysterical one. She could still have her life and her friendships. It would be a wonderful 4 years for her. She could go and do anything she wanted to. He was a shoe in to win and she was still a beautiful counterpart. She knew the game and how to play it. She even turned a blind eye to Lady even though he knew she would have liked to see him with a more "conservative" –wealthy partner. At his age, he didn't want conservative, he wanted spice! Lady was pure spice and excitement to him. Her skin was like electric velvet. He couldn't get enough of her. "Oh my God, I don't know how to keep her now!" he realized in dismay. How could he keep her? They'd ruin him over her, they'd ruin *her*. He remembered her saying that she thought someone was following her last week, someone was giving her a hard time. Is that what this was all about. They were driving her away so he would have a clear shot at being

Mayor? "That's ridiculous!" he thought as he thumbed through his schedule for the coming week. It was the same old thing, luncheons, dinner parties and community meetings. He had one on schedule right now. He grabbed his jacket and headed out the door to the lower lobby of the Sicktowne Library. Outside he stopped at his new Jeep—like all the town and county cars it was courtesy of "Reds Car" and he decided to walk the 2 blocks over to try and clear his head. He checked his cell phone and saw that Lady had called him four times. "That's unusual," he thought. "I wonder what's up." The Rainmaker was already at the back entrance to the Library and as he dialed the phone to call Lady, he grabbed his elbow. He hung up his phone before it connected and thought to himself "She knows I'm busy. I'll call her later on." They hustled into the Library to field more questions at the community meeting about the new Majestic building project. "Ugh" he said to the Rainmaker, "Right now I could use some of that sweet wine you always offer." "Oh, I have a flask in my pocket. Stop off at the little boys room and collect yourself. Here." he pushed the silver flask into his jacket pocket. "I'll be right back." he marched into the men's room and locked the door. Something was nagging at him to call Lady. He dialed her and she sounded weepy. "What's wrong honey?" he asked. "Oh sweetie, it's a horrible day!" Lady moaned. "I've had a fight with my daughter and she moved out! Someone was following her and tormenting her for months and now they're doing it to me all the time! What am I going to do? I haven't been out of the house for days!" she started to cry hard now. The Advisor spoke soothingly, "Try to calm down honey, are you sure you're being followed? Have you been to the Dr. lately? Are you taking anything now? Did you call your Therapist?" She had told him that she was seeing a Therapist years ago to get through her divorce. "I'm not crazy!" Lady shouted. "This is really happening! Oh my God,

can't you understand what is happening to me!"
she shouted. "Lady, calm down, I can't do
anything about it now, I'm heading into a
community meeting. I've got a hundred people
waiting on me!" he responded. He was
flabbergasted at what she was telling him. "Take
something to calm yourself down. We'll work on it
in the morning. This meeting is going to run late,"
he could hear Lady sobbing on the other end of the
phone. "okay," Lady whispered. "Maybe later,"
she said quietly. He heard the click as she hung up
on him. He stood in front of the washbasin mirror
and took a drink from the flask. "This was some
day, so much junk to wade through, and now this."
He opened the door and looked for the Trustee that
the insiders called the "Rainmaker." They knew he
was part owner of a Long Island vineyard. He was
making a fortune on the bars and restaurants that
they'd been moving into town over the past 2
years. They all had to agree to buy all their wine
from him or they weren't gonna stay in business in

his town for long. Like the Advisor, he was gonna make a fortune at the Majestic bar and night club when it opened next year. He was waiting for him to go down the long staircase to the meeting.

Chapter 12

The new 'Advisor'

Mickey was amazed by all of the fanfare at the "coming out party." He had watched Emerald move through each part of her ceremony with poise and grace. To please her Mother she had donned a pair of wrist high white gloves. With her beautiful emerald green dress and white gloves, the photographer had her recreate poses so that her pictures would resemble her Mothers from 50 years ago. It was charming to see the 2 of them together and everyone commented on how beautiful Emerald would be when she got older because her Mother remained so lovely. "If you want to know what the girl will look like in 20 years, look at the Mother," one of the garden party ladies had chided as she poked him in the ribs. Red must have sent the word out to the entire room, Mickey had thought to himself. He should have known. As the party dispersed he found himself alone with Emerald and he was once again slightly edgy with her. "You look beautiful today," he stammered. "Why thank you, so do you," she giggled. He was surprised at her flirtation. "You won't mind if I accompany you home would you? I'm invited to the after party." "Oh that's great," she gushed. "You can meet my court. They came over last night and decorated the lawn with a Fall theme for fun. My Jeep was made to look like a Pumpkin this morning. They had these big orange styrofoam cut-outs on the front and back. Mom was delighted. Dad wants to park it in front of the dealership for a sales pitch. He said his sales go up every time he has a gimmick attached to the campaign. He's gonna use the slogan "We'll turn your pumpkin into a beautiful carriage," to push out the old inventory to the graduating High School Seniors so he can move the new stuff in after January. It's Fall ya' know so it's the big push for the beginning of the end of the year clearance." He was shocked and relieved to hear how much she knew about how her Fathers business ran. "That's great Em," he called out. "Did you have a great day?" he asked as he stepped closer to her and looked down into her cherubish face. "It was wonderful, wasn't it? Could a girl ask for more?" She was grinning from ear to ear as she twisted the thick satin ribbon on her dress. "It sure was," he gently lifted her chin as if he was going to kiss her lips. He could see the startled look in her eyes so he veered to the left and kissed her gently on her warm cheek. "You better get going, I can see your Dad is waiting for you," he glanced over towards where Red was standing by the doorway. He was giving Mickey a hard stare. "I'll see you at the house," she said as she walked towards Red. Mickey followed her slowly and made his way past the group of family and court that had surrounded her and Red. He sat in his car for a while going over the conversation with Emerald in his mind. He was satisfied with the exchange. He hadn't choked or sweated profusely like a school boy. He was a grown man and all that was nonsense to him, he hated to recall the times he felt terribly uncomfortable around Emerald. He had never had this much trouble warming up to a female before. Maybe it was knowing that she would be the Mother of his children that put him on edge. That was something he had never considered with any other woman. He reached for his phone to call Lady. He wanted her advice before he headed over to the after party. He was dialing as he drove to the local burger joint, a drive thru Vanilla shake was on his mind. Lady was a mess, crying over her daughter and going on hysterically about people following her so he cut the call short and headed to the party. The house was lit with a beautiful decoration of white lights in the trees. He could see the Fall décor that Emerald had told him about, and her Pumpkin car. He knew he was going to get a razzing about his foreign car. Taboo in this town, "Reds Car" only sold American made automobiles.

His dealership supplied all the Town and County Politician cars as well as the Post Office vehicles, the water company and the County Detectives. All the government and civil service contracts went to all American made "Reds Car." His Buggatti was the envy of his friends though and this always brought a smile to his face. The few friends he kept had all settled down and were doing what he called the "mortgage battle" these days. The 9-5 and home to the house full of kids kept them chained to their routines. He could come and go and afford the Buggatti, his salary at his job was tripled because his Father owned the fire equipment company. He could hear the laughter and tinkle of glasses as he approached the house. The Fall evening was presenting a glorious sunset and the last rays had gone. He knew better than to ring the bell and he pushed the white wooden door inwards to step into the Foyer. The house staff was waiting to take his coat and he waved hello to Effy the Housekeeper. She looked flushed and excited.

"Mr. Mickey," she drawled. Lola had brought Effy with her when she moved from the South. Effy knew how to run the household "with Southern charm" Lola always said. The High Schoolers were singing in the large family room. A karaoke machine was blasting the latest hit. The room had 3 large screen televisions and some of the group was staring at the Karaoke TV, others were staring at the MTV screen and the third television was running a PowerPoint montage of pictures of Emerald and her family through the years. There were about 90 kids in all and every one of them was eating something. The 'grown ups' –"oh my God I'm old" he thought to himself, were out back on the deck hovering near the fire pit and outdoor heaters. Emerald saw him out of the corner of her eye and he gave a wave that pointed to the deck. She made a thumbs up sign and waved back as she mouthed the work "Later" into the air. Lola was surrounded by her camp near the fire pit, Red was at the bar. He eased his way through the crowd of

200 and made his way over to Lola. She blew him a kiss and when he got closer, she handed him a glass of cold champagne. "Beautiful day wasn't it Mickey," she said as he sipped his glass and gave her his "charming eyes." "No harm in flirting with Lola," he thought "keep me in her mind, thinking what a catch I would be for Em." "You deserve all the best days Lola" he replied. "Isn't Emerald so grown up though! I didn't see any boyfriends hovering around, what's her plan after High School?" "She wants to go to work for her Daddy! Or at least that's how she feels this week. I don't particularly like the idea but she's always known her own mind and until she changes it, she will do as she pleases. I don't see how she's going to meet a quality man up North. I guess I did but then again I've always been a very lucky woman." Mickey bowed his head lower for maximum eye contact and in his most gracious voice he said

"Lola, you are presently looking into the eyes of a quality man my lady and I hope you will recommend me to your beautiful daughter as it is my intention to begin to court her." Lola's eyes flew wide and her mouth dropped open. "Mickey! You can't mean it?" she replied incredulously. "What can I say?" she stammered, "Does Red approve?" He had finished his champagne and as the server moved through he placed his empty glass on the tray and took 2 fresh glasses, one for himself and he handed the other to Lola. "Cheers," he called out as he touched her glass with his, "Red was made aware of my hopes and dreams just this afternoon. He did not put up a fight." He smiled widely. "Well then, welcome to the family darlin'" Lola purred as she placed her hand into the crook of his elbow to warm it. "Let's drink to my daughters' happiness. You know what they say where I come from – 'you've got to get your Possum while you're still in blossom!' and my baby is about to bloom!" They laughed and began to sway as the music for the evening began to play. Just then Emerald stepped onto the patio. As she made her way towards her Mother and Mickey, she stopped for hugs and snippets of conversation from her guests. "Hi Mom" she gushed as she grabbed Lola and rubbed her face into her Mother's champagne flushed cheek. She moved on to Mickey, awkward for a moment and then she wrapped her arms around his neck and tiptoed up to softly kiss his mouth. He had instinctively placed his left hand on her low back, the champagne glass was balanced in his right. He thought to himself "Oh my gosh, if my hand was empty I would have pulled her towards me and kissed her hard! I would have blown it on the first public outing!" Instead he smiled at her and moved his left hand up to tousle the back of her long beautiful strawberry blond hair. It was soft and he twirled the ends around his finger and brought it to rest under her nose like a mustache. It tickled her and she giggled. He said "You look quite fetching with your mustache Em don't you think?" She was still giggling and he took her hand and brought it to his mouth to kiss it. He had placed the champagne glass on the table and he pulled her hand towards his shoulder and began to slowly sway dance to the music with her. The crowd took a half step back and a few flashes from cellphones captured the image and Emerald was awe struck at how easily Mickey took command of her body and began to swing waltz her around in a small circle. She felt perfectly natural with him and she felt herself fall hard for him in that moment. She was afraid at the power of her emotions and she was swimming in the smell of his cologne, it was seducing her senses. Lola watched her daughter and knew she had met her life mate. She felt a pang of fear at losing "her girl" and she reacted by lightly applauding the dancers and she had to sit down to accept the scene that was unfolding in front of her. The crowd joined her applause and Mickey knew he had captured Emerald, he gave her a gentle twirl and bowed to end the spell. More pictures and applause and he stood a foot away facing her and gave Emerald his sexiest grin. Emerald took two steps toward Lola swung her feet up and sat on her lap. Like a toddler who was flustered and ran back to the safety of her Mama's lap. Everyone laughed to see Emerald transform from a young woman to a little girl in the space of 10 minutes. She blushed and pushed her face into her Mothers hair and Mickey leaned in to pick up his glass to sip casually. He saw Red watching the whole exchange and he sensed that Emerald was bewildered so he headed over and shook Reds hand with a knowing look in his eyes. Red clapped him on the back and said "I think my daughter just gave her heart away." Mickey replied, "I hope you won't mind if I ask her out for next Saturday night, Red. I'm heading out to one of the vineyards for a Gala and she's going to need an evening dress. She might want to put her hair up. Now that I think of it she might need a few new dresses for the evenings I've got planned." Red chided him "Don't think about introducing my girl to the drink now Mickey, she's still just a slip of a girl and I'm not keen on polluting her so young." "I would never think of it Red. She's too sweet to spoil. She'll always be safe with me, I can assure you of that." Red shook his head as he looked seriously at Lola and said "Well man, you'll have to see if she'll go out with you won't you." "We'll see," said Mickey. "Have you heard from the Advisor today? I heard a rumor and I wonder if you got a phone call. They've planned for him to be Mayor and if you're serious about my Emerald, you might consider coming on board as his replacement. What do you say? Mickey recoiled as if Red had struck him. He had never considered anything political. His heart was racing and he felt his hand rub his forehead as if to wipe away the shock. "I won't say no," was all he could manage to squawk out. They watched Lola push Em off and heard her say, "Sweetie, my legs can't hold you much longer, you really have grown!" The guests had gathered around them for chatter and the servers were moving through the crowd with delicious smelling treats. The decorative orange and white patio lights came on and everyone said "oooh" and Emeralds court came out and lined up for more "fun poses" with her. The kids were giggling and making funny faces and the crowd laughed at their entertainment. Mickey wished he was young again.

Chapter 13

Mickey got home late. Much too late to call Lady. He was pleased with himself and he knew that he had hit a home run at Emeralds party last night. He smiled as he remembered the way she had approached him as he was leaving. She had fixed his collar and straightened his tie like a doting wife. He had won her! She was so young, she had been like ripened fruit hanging from the branch. So sweet! He was thumbing through his mail over coffee and he was curious about a letter from Lady. What he read when he opened it was shocking. The letter was a copy of a complaint form that Lady had filled out and filed with the fraud department of the Attorney General of New York State. She was claiming that a mortgage broker from Sicktowne was buying and selling her mortgage back and forth with the local Home dispatch store and raising her payments until she couldn't afford them anymore. She mentioned a fraud scam to modify her mortgage that allowed them to collect all of her personal and financial information and finally, she claimed to be the victim of Identity Theft. She had hand written note to Mickey that said, "Hi my sweet man, please follow through with this for me. I've sent a box of original documents over to you with the complaint form. You're a great Lawyer and I know you will be able to figure this all out better than I ever could. I hope you will always take care of my daughter, she's yours too you know. Remember the night at The Point with the big bonfire? We were young and beautiful like she is now. I love you, I always will. Love, Lady. Mickey re-read the letter 5 times and was stunned by the news of his daughter with Lady. He felt the wind knocked out of him and he held onto the small breakfast table to take the spin out of his head. "Can this be real?" he thought. "I was so drunk the night of the bonfire that I never realized it was Lady who was undressing me. She had just married that loser husband of hers and I was so angry with her!" As his head hung low he saw the brown box on the chair next to him. It was addressed by Lady, the same as the letter had been. It must be the documents she sent over. His mind was racing through the years of all the memories that he had of "Baby Lady," he thought it was cute that Lady had named her baby after herself. Lady always brought her over to his place when she visited. "Look how beautiful Baby Lady is!" she would squeal with delight. He understood so much more now. They had many hours of playtime with "Baby Lady" and he truly loved the girl as a "niece." He wasn't even her Godfather for God's sake he found himself thinking. He tried to call Lady but she wasn't answering. He was moving around his apartment in a kind of trance. One minute happy to have a daughter, the next angry that Lady had let so much time go by without telling him. His phone rang and it was the Advisor. He knew he had to take the call, even though it had come at the worst time. "Hello," he said sounding annoyed. "Hey Mickey!" the Advisor shouted. "Long time no hear from buddy. How's things going in the 'Land of Linen'." "What?" Mickey asked. "That's what they're calling that place nowadays, you up to meeting for some coffee around the corner?" "Not really, not right now," Mickey announced, he realized he wasn't gonna be good for anything else today. The Advisor said, "Well you know my schedule does not allow for a lot of free time so I'm gonna have to do this on the phone then." Mickey already knew what he was going to say. "Normally, I'd have a face to face and give you the razzle dazzle Mick," he started. "No problem, I'm a big boy, I can handle it," Mickey replied. "Ok then, you wanna come on board as the Advisor when I get the Mayors job next year?" Mickey did his best to sound surprised. "Wow, you really pack a punch there guy. I'm a little overwhelmed to say the least. Wow and congratulations to you!" The Advisor was walking out of the coffee shop and heading South on Jane Street. He was heading straight for Mickeys place. "Yea well, it was a surprise to me too. I gotta do it so I thought I'd get the best friend I have to do the job with me." He pushed the elevator button to the 5th floor to knock at Mickeys door. "I'm your friend either way Mickey and I could use your help to keep things on track in this town and to get the Majestic building up." He was knocking on Mickeys door. "Hold on, I gotta get the door." Mickey was so used to living in the building alone that he didn't even realize that the doorbell didn't ring. He was so upset that he didn't bother with the peep hole, he just threw the door open wide. "Hey ya punk!" The Advisor swung his arm to place a pretend punch on Mickeys head. "Oh man!" Mickey hollered out. "You know you got me, I can't say no to you!" They bumped chests in a fake hug. The Advisor followed Mickey to the kitchen. Mickey offered him a coffee. "We should have champagne!" Mickey said as he opened his refrigerator. "I need a drink!" Mickey popped the cork and was serving the Advisor when he said "It's going to be a beautiful four years." Mickey had pushed the letter from Lady under his bill pile as he went to the door. He had flipped the box full of documents upside down to hide the address label with the handwriting on it. They were at the patio window overlooking the town. "How appropriate," the Advisor said out loud. I couldn't have planned it any better, he thought. After a long pause he said "Well Mick, I gotta go, I gotta run all over town as usual." Mickey said "Let me know what comes next." "Will do," the Advisor chimed as he slipped on his jacket. "Have you heard from Lady?" he asked. "No, I was just trying to call her when you came over. What's going on with her? She was pretty upset last night. She said the neighbors in Kingdom Lake were giving her a hard time or something." The Advisor let out a sigh and moved towards the door. "She was out of her mind last night when she called me and I can't reach her so I'm going to head over to see her right after this meeting with my wife.

Chapter 14

A "new" Administration

Mickey waved the Advisor off and went back to re-read the letter from Lady. It still hadn't registered right in his mind. What was this letter to the Attorney General all about? He tried to call her again and again there was no answer. That was unusual for Lady, she was taking his calls all the time now and she was letting him know that she was always home and always afraid. He decided to drive to see her now. He dressed quickly and headed down to the garage for the 6 minute drive to her house. It was always dim in the garage over the past few weeks more and more cars were parking in his area. "New neighbors, I never see them," he thought as he walked. He was startled by a shadow near his car. A figure stepped out, a man wearing a grey wool coat walked towards him. "We were just heading up Mickey." It was the local Detective. The town hired him to "blend in" and keep an eye on everything that went on in the town, he had sources everywhere. "What's up Lou?" "Hey, Mick, I'm so sorry buddy, I'm so sorry to tell ya about Lady," he said softly as he grabbed Mickeys elbow. Mickey stared at him and waited. "Yea, we got a call at the precinct this morning, she, she didn't make it Mick. She's gone." Mickey felt his knees give out and Lou grabbed him by both arms to keep him standing. He gave out a muffled moan as he stuffed his fist into his mouth to block the sound. Lou half pushed, half dragged him over to sit him down on the hood of the Buggatti. Mickeys chin was on his chest and he started heaving with sobs. "How?" he asked. "It's okay, it's okay," Lou kept saying, "She took some pills and went to bed. That's all we know right now." Mickey stopped sobbing and got quiet. "I gotta go upstairs Lou. I gotta get myself together." They walked towards the elevator and back up to the apartment. "I'm okay," Mickey said as they got to his door. His hand shook as he pushed his key into the lock. "You sure Mickey, you sure you're ok? I can come in for a while. I can stay and help ya. Call me if you need something." Lou said softly. Mickey silently closed the door and dragged himself over to the couch to cry. After about an hour he recovered enough of his senses to use his cellphone to call the Advisor. His call went to voicemail and he knew better than to leave a message. The Advisor was staring at the phone but couldn't take the call. He was sitting in the office of the Rainmaker going over folders full of paperwork that they had filed for fake corporations under Lady's name. She was wealthy and didn't know it. The Advisor and the Rainmaker were partners for years and Lady was the perfect "Muppet." She had no family and very few close friends. The only person they ever had to look out for was Mickey. He had no idea of what they were doing as they funneled the money through lady and into their pockets. Neither did she. Now, they had to liquidate everything in a hurry. They had found out about Lady an hour ago when Lou, the town Detective called. Lady was gone and nothing would bring her back. The Advisor was distraught and the only other person who knew about the money laundering was the Rainmaker. He was drawing up a false will as the Advisor combed through the folders for information. 15 companies in all had to be re-worked. They would have to absorb the costs and taxes unless they could figure out a way to combine it all and push it on to the new Majestic Building. It would mean starting out the building "in the red" but the amount of money that was going to be generated would make up for it inside of 6 months. The only way to do it would be to move everything into the only other person who had her name, Lady's daughter. She had just turned 18 so they could simply change the date of birth and refile the paperwork with last weeks' date on it. One week before her death, Lady would have transferred ownership to her daughter, Lady.

Females had no "junior" attached so the transition would be seamless. They had run her daughter out of town and she wouldn't know what to do even if she was still around Sicktowne. Finally done, the Advisor handed everything to the Rainmaker and grabbed his coat. "We still might make some money to cover everything," the Rainmaker quipped, "Last year I took a life insurance policy out on her to the tune of 1 million dollars. It will only cover half, unless we can prove that her death was an accidental overdose. I'll have the boys at the Precinct fix it up. They'll dig up a Pharmacy record that shows she was given two legit prescriptions for meds that shouldn't ever be taken together. She took 'em and it was lethal Problem solved." The Advisor hung his head and answered "Whatever." "Sorry" the Rainmaker said softly, "I forgot how much you liked her. I've got another that will cheer you up when you're ready." The Advisor shook his hand and headed home. "Nothing about Politics is pretty." He thought as he left. "This time next year I'll be Mayor with a whole new administration to do all the work and I can begin to plan my retirement again."

Made in the USA
Charleston, SC
28 July 2014